SELF IMPROVEMENT
CREDIT
REPAIR MANUAL

SELF IMPROVEMENT
CREDIT
REPAIR MANUAL

YOU ARE NOT ALONE

VALERIE JOHNSON

SELF IMPROVEMENT CREDIT REPAIR MANUAL
YOU ARE NOT ALONE

iUniverse books may be ordered through booksellers or by contacting:

iUniverse
1663 Liberty Drive
Bloomington, IN 47403
www.iuniverse.com
844-349-9409

ISBN: 978-1-6632-5383-5 (sc)
ISBN: 978-1-6632-5382-8 (e)

Library of Congress Control Number: 2023911312

Print information available on the last page.

iUniverse rev. date: 06/15/2023

DEDICATION

My name is Ms. Valerie Wilson Johnson. I am the Best-Selling Author of this Self Improvement Credit Repair Manual. I am dedicating this Self Improvement Credit Repair Manual to my Heroes. This Book is dedicated to my Heroes my Dad who passed away April 1ˢᵗ, 2023, My Son Eric who passed away January 19, 2022, my friend Tony Lowe who passed away January 29, 2023, I love and I Miss You. Thank You for believing in me.

This Book is dedicated to everyone Who has less than perfect credit and for those who wants self-Improvement and Better Credit Scores. I dedicate this Book to You! Mom, Anthony, Tiara, Jocelynn Armani, Family, Friends, Instructor Sheila, Sorority Sisters, Soror Lamae, Soror Patty, Soror Grace, Soror Tricia, Church Friends, Shamelia Rogers, Valerie Stitt, and my Biological Sisters and Brothers, Denise, Jennifer, Vallana, Vanessa, Darien, Isaac, and to my nieces Brooke, Blair, and Nephew Blake and Sister in Love Katrina.

You all inspire me to self-improve and to not Limit Gods Possibilities in My life and career. God Is Able! Live Long And Prosper!

FOREWORD

The Self Improvement Credit Repair Manual was a wonderful innovative step by step process on building and establishing strong credit. In homebuying credit plays a important piece in determining which programs people qualify for, what interest rate they receive and what downpayment will be required of them. If consumers follow the steps communicated in this manual it will greatly enhance their financial futures and their paths to homeownership.

Saleem Shabazz
Community Development Loan Officer

I really enjoyed reading your book!

"Valerie is very passionate and intentional about educating others on repairing and building their credit. This is book is relevant and practical. It is a must read!"

Kelly Dockery M&T Bank

PREFACE/MISSION STATEMENT

Hi, my Name is Ms. Valerie Wilson Johnson. The title of this book is Self-Improvement Credit Repair Manual, and You are Not Alone!

This Self Improvement Credit Repair Manual is on the topic of Credit. This Manual is for ages 16 to 90 although most credit applicants are 18 and older. I promise you this Credit Repair Manual will help individuals, families, and Small Business Owners to improve their Credit Score. I hope you will enjoy reading this helpful information!

Just a FYI I do not discriminate. Happy Reading! My mission statements!" THE AMERICAN DREAM IS OBTAINABLE. Just Start Self Improving. It is up to God and You!

ACKNOWLEDGEMENT
WHO HELPED IN CREATING OF THIS BOOK

I want to Acknowledge My Lord and Savior, and Deliverer Jesus Christ. Our inspiration and Visionary Sheila L Brown Director of SLB Author Academy and to my inspirational fellow classmates and Sisters and brother in Christ and I want to acknowledge my encouragers and Director and co-workers, and our beneficiaries of Salvation Army ARC. May God Bless You! Thank You.

INTRODUCTION

You are not alone. According to Capital One 1 out of 4 Americans have a Credit Score of 580 or below. This Credit Repair Manual Is a helpful tool for those who may have a lower Credit Score. This Credit Repair Manual is for those whose goals are to improve his or hers credit score from Bad to Fair to Good to Excellent reported credit. With God All Things Are Possible. Start paying your bills on time today!

Congratulations on making steps towards your improved Credit Score. This Author went from a 498 to 643 Credit Score! You can do it! You can self-improve your credit scores.

Questions You Should Be Asking Yourself. What are my Credit Scores from the three bureaus? What are my Dream Scores?

There are steps to repairing your poor or less than perfect credit scores. You may feel overwhelmed at times but there are steps to repairing your personal credit profile. This self-improvement credit repair manual is just that. This credit repair manual is going to provide a step-by-step guide to obtaining your dream credit score, step by step.

If you utilize this Self Improvement Credit Repair Manual, you will improve your credit score and from month to month you will see an increase in your credit score as you pay your bills in a timely manner. Self-improvement can be easy, and you are not alone. This Credit Repair Manual can be used as a tool and upon completion you will have the tools needed to obtain secured credit cards, unsecured credit, cars and on your way to the Ultimate Self Improvement HOMEOWNERSHIP! You Can Do It. Philippians 4:13, Says I can do all things through Christ who strengthens me.

Questions to Ask Your self. Although I am in debt, How many points am I away from my Dream Credit Scores.

Valerie Johnson

NOTES

_____

_____

_____

_____

_____

_____

_____

_____

_____

_____

_____

_____

_____

Valerie Johnson

Put a smile on your face. You are blessed. Increased Credit Scores does take time, but believe in yourself, and start today! This Self Improvement manual will help you to obtain the Joy and Blessing of being able to obtain Credit Cards, Cars, Mortgage and your 1st time Homeownership. Believe me I am excited for you the reader of this Manual. There are helpful tools included in this Self Improvement Credit Repair Manual. You will get examples of helpful letters from How to Dispute, Sample Letters, to Simple Bill Payment Schedules for helpful month to month payment of bills.

Credit Repair challenges negative items on your credit report. This Credit Report Manual will show you how to dispute the right way. Negative items effect your credit score including hard inquires in a derogatory way. Another word for derogatory is negative. Just a FYI on your credit repair there are Positive and sometimes although we do not like it, there are negative items and sometimes it is either not our information, or more than 7 years old.

This Self Improvement Credit Repair Manual provides letters to help you on the way to Good Credit. This Manual is a good read and this manual I guarantee will help you correct incorrect info by encouraging you to REQUEST YOUR ANNUAL REPORT YEARLY, FOR FREE. You can also buy your two additional reports. Another way of obtaining your Credit Report for free is a request after your credit was denied. When denied Credit, you may request a report from the reported Credit Bureau who the denial was reported to. This report is Free!!!!

There are 3 Bureaus the names of the Three Credit Bureaus are Equifax, Experian and Trans Union Credit Bureaus.

Some Credit and US Statistics. According to Bank rate, LLC a consumer financial services company based in NYC, statistics says Credit Card debt is on the rise. American card balances reached $986 Billion! In 2022 according to Federal Reserve Bank of New York. The average credit card debt in the USA an Experian source says it is $5,221. The Average credit Utilization rate was 25.6% and the average credit cards an American person averages is the number 3.84%.

Let's talk averages for a minute. The average past due delinquency rates are 30-59 days past due at a rate of 1.04%. Experian also reported that despite the pandemic beginning 2020 to this present time the average credit score increased at least 4 points in 2021. Credit scores have been steadily increasing since the Great Recession a total increase of 25 points.

According to a reliable source Experian, Generation x ages 41-56 had the largest amount of credit card debt at $7,070.00. At the lowest amount of credit card debt owed Generation Z 18-24 $2,282.00. Wow!

According to Federal Reserve's report on the Economic wellbeing of the U.S. Households in 2021 published in May 2022, despite carrying lower credit card balances Black and Hispanics are less to be approved credit compared to White, Asians. However, I believe God and I believe in Change.

Valerie Johnson

SAMPLE LETTERS TO EQUIFAX

P.O. BOX 740241
Atlanta, Georgia
30374-0241

Dear Sir/Madam

    My Name is _____. I am requesting a free copy of my Annual Credit Report. I reside at _____ in _____, _____.

    The last four digits of my social security number are _____. Please send my free copy of my Equifax Credit Report to _____. Enclosed is a copy of my state Identification.

Salutation,

Name _____

SAMPLE LETTERS TO EXPERIAN

Experian
PO Box 2104
Allen, Texas 75013-0949

Dear Sir/Madam

 I am requesting a free copy of my credit report. My name is_____.
My address is _____, City, State and zip code.
 The last four digits of my social security number are_____. Please send
a copy of my free Experian Credit Report to my mailing address provided.
Enclosed is a copy of my state Identification.

Salutation,

Name

Please note you can request only one free Annual Credit Report. Additional
Bureaus cost a small fee. Unless denied credit.

SAMPLE LETTER TO TRANSUNION

Trans Union
PO Box 1000
Chester, PA 19022

Dear Sir/Madam

    I am requesting a free copy of my Trans Union Credit Report. My name is _____. I reside at _____, City, State, and Zip code_____.

    The last four digits of my Social Security Numbers are _____. Please send a copy of my free Trans Union Report to the address provided. Enclosed is a copy of my state Identification.

Salutation,

Please Note you can only request one free report. Additional bureaus are a small fee unless you were denied credit.

I WAS DENIED CREDIT LETTER

Name
Address
City, State, Zip code

Dear Sir/Madam

I was denied credit. I received a denial letter or email. I am requesting a copy of my free Credit Report Please.

My name is _____. My address is _____ City, State, and Zip code. The last four digits of my social security number is _____. Enclosed is a copy of my state issued Identification.

Please mail my free copy of my credit report to _____, City, State, and Zip code.

Salutation,

Name

Valerie Johnson

Monthly Planner

Month

Year

Goals of the Month

Week 1

Week 2

Week 3

Week 4

Week 5

Progress Report

Total Tasks

Total Achieved

Percent Achieved

Grade Yourself

NOTES

_____

_____

_____

_____

_____

_____

_____

_____

_____

_____

_____

_____

_____

Valerie Johnson

3

Godliness is a great source of profit when it is combined with what you already have 1 Timothy 6:6

Your credit score requires work? These are some helps!

1. Spending 30% or less of your Credit Limit.
2. For an even better score 10% of your credit limit.
3. Limit the amount of credit applications you apply for.
4. Keep up good payment history. Long term good payment history is a plus. Please note it is never too late to begin paying on time. Timely payments equal a better credit score.
5. Communicate with your creditor, especially if you need to change your bill payment date to your payday.

Valerie Johnson

NOTES

Valerie Johnson

4

WHAT FICO MEANS AND ITS DERIVATIVE.

In 1989 Fico introduced then called Fair Isaac Corporation. The Fico is a model used by most banks and credit grantors and is based on the consumer credit files of the 3 Credit Bureaus.

A fico score creates a variety of credit scores for use by lenders, credit card issuers, and other creditors. Fico scores range from 300 a poor score to 850 an excellent score. Your fico score is determined if your application is approved and according to the APR rate you are offered. Credit APR ranges from to. APR rates are determined by your credit score.

The fico score is made up of

1. <u>Payment History 35%</u> A brief explanation. Payment history is one of the ways your credit score can improve. Meaning, paying your bills on time and before the requested amount due date and I must add communication with Creditors is very important.
2. <u>Amount Owed is</u> the 30% of your score. Please note the amount owed is the amount you currently owe the Creditor and Lenders.

3. <u>Length of Credit History</u> 15% of your fico score. Please note the longer you have had a credit account the better your Fico Score.
4. <u>Credit Mix</u> Equals 10% of your Credit Score.
5. <u>New Credit</u> Equals 10% of your Credit Score

Valerie Johnson

EXAMPLE OF A GOOD CREDIT MIX

3 to 5 Credit Cards

A Car Payment

A Mortgage or Reported Rent Payment whether it is a 1/1 Arm Mortgage, 10/1 Arm or a 30-year fixed Mortgage. This is an example of a Credit Mix.

Question

What is your Credit Mix?

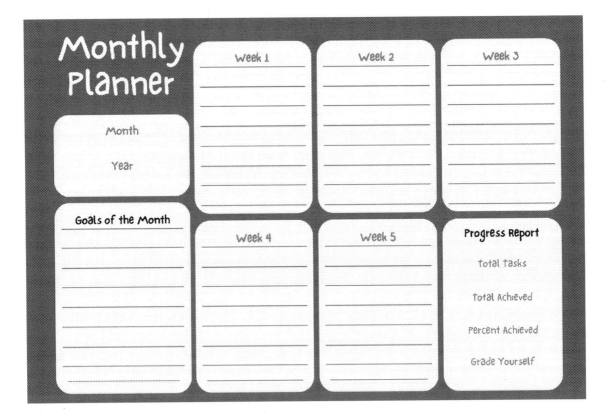

Valerie Johnson

NOTES

_____

_____

_____

_____

_____

_____

_____

_____

_____

_____

_____

_____

_____

_____

5

REASON FOR THIS SELF IMPROVEMENT CREDIT REPAIR BOOK.

This Author has had to learn how to read her credit report and found mistakes and inaccurate or even reported info 7 years or older on my report at various times in my life. Consumer Protection bureaus may not report negative information more than seven years old or bankrupt more than 10 years old. The good news is the law is designed not to punish you for past mistakes due to circumstances.

Although I have been blessed not to have gone Bankrupt, I have had inaccuracies that from a period of tome unknowingly prevented me from achieving goals including 1st time Homeownership, my #1 goal. It is never too late to achieve, your homeownership goal.

I participated in Credit Repair programs only to become disappointed with in addition to the Credit Repair Program. In fact, I paid monthly fees equally up to hundreds of dollars and did not receive the results I was looking for. So I started doing Credit Repair myself and am seeing some results.

If this is your story let me help you to obtain your goal of reaching your dream credit scores, one month at a time. I want to help you with your

Self-improvement read this Credit Repair Manual Cover to Cover. This Credit Repair Manual Can Help You!

Not only is the Author working toward improving her credit I believe in God! Ephesians 3:20 Says, Our God can Do Exceedingly Abundantly Above All We Can Ask or Think! Believe and Do the Work!

You can obtain your dream of becoming approved for a car with income and less than perfect credit. A shout out to Roman at 716 Automotive Credit. I thank God for Humble beginnings. Oh and for a start a Credit Card! There is a company who usually gives people with less than perfect Credit approvals for Credit Card Credit. The company name is Credit One. You might have to begin with a $300.00 credit limit. But a WIN is a WIN!

You can get the address and email address for credit card applications in Chapter 10 of this book. Happy reading be encouraged, be optimistic nor pessimistic you're going to use the tools and information provided and you are going to improve your credit score one month at a time.

Some important information for you the reader of these book. Give yourself 120 days for your Credit Score to improve. You can call the bureau and request a Credit freeze, just simply means I am not applying for no more credit at this time. Great tool especially for someone who feel they are a victim of Identity theft.

Valerie Johnson

NOTES

6

I WANT TO IMPROVE MY CREDIT SCORES!
WHAT DO I DO! YOU CAN SELF IMPROVE!

1. Simply Challenge Negative Items on Your Credit Report
2. The Reason is Negative derogative items effects your Credit Score Including Hard Inquiries
3. Reduce Your Number of Inquiries. Inquiries stay on your report for over two years.

According to Capital One Hard Inquiries are taking are taken off your credit report after two years. But you can request to have inquiries removed off your credit report in a DISPUTE LETTER! An FYI Soft Inquiries won't affect your credit scores and example is a pre-approval!

Hard Inquires happen when a lender or credit card company checks your credit for the purpose of possible Approval.

Soft Inquiries occur when a person or company checks you as part of a background check. Soft Inquiries won't affect your credit score.

This Authors goal is to motivate you to help you to utilize the information in this Self Improvement Credit Repair Manual! This manual provides samples

Valerie Johnson

of sample dispute letters that you read. The goal is to know what is on your credit reports and the goal is to get the negative information removed, by providing proof and substantiating your challenge or dispute or by a letter from the Creditor.

Most Americans work hard, and it is unfair but not unusual to see an inaccuracy on your report. Challenge in accuracy and you can improve your credit scores.

7

GLOSSARY OF IMPORTANT TERMS

1/1 Arm
Adjustable – rate Mortgage
Set interest rate first year, after period rate adjust yearly

10/1 Arm
An adjustable – rate mortgage set interest rate first 10 years after that period adjust yearly

3 in 1 Credit Report
Credit Report, this type of report includes TransUnion, Experian and Equifax

ACH
Transferring of Funds

Valerie Johnson

Electronically between business, consumers and Financial Institutions

Annual Credit Report.com
An official website for obtaining your free Credit Reports you have the right to obtain yearly. Free Service does not include scores

Annual Fee
A charge usually yearly ranging between $10-$50 yearly.

Annual Percentage Rate
(APR)

Interest Rate Being Charged on Debt (Balanced Owed) FYI Credit Cards have one for purchase, one for cash advance and one for Balance Transfers

Application Fee
A charge to submit a credit card application. Amount lender charges to process your loan documents

Asset
Things owned by a person that have cash Value an Example Car, Home, Boats, Savings, Investments

Beacon Score
Name of Fico Score from Equifax

Biweekly Mortgage
Schedules Payments every two weeks instead of monthly payments

Borrower
Individual requesting Loan, responsible party the debt

Cardholder
Person issued the credit card

Closing Cost
Amounts charged the consumer. Closing cost include Lender, title, escrow fees 3-6% of purchase price

Collections is when original creditor sells debt in order to collect money owed

Cosigner
Equal responsible for a debt

Credit File
Another file for Credit Report

Credit Freeze
A request to ask the Credit bureau from refraining from sharing a consumer's credit report with any third parties

Credit History
Info on a Credit Report record of how you paid past bills

Credit Limit
The Amount you're allowed to spend in Credit granted.

Valerie Johnson

NOTES

Valerie Johnson

8

EXAMPLES OF HOW TO IMPROVE CREDIT IN THIS CREDIT REPAIR MANUAL

This Credit Repair Manual will get you in the practice of verifying then correcting incorrect information on your report and by paying all your bills on time and above the requests amount asked by your creditor.

An Example

Ms. Johnson receives her credit card statement. She has spent $70.00 30% of usage and her payment is due on the 7th. On the 5th she pays payment they asked for plus an additional $10.00 dollars. The credit company asked for $10.00 in the credit card statement. Minimum due is $10.00 she the credit card holder, paid $20.00. All correct steps to good credit. Steps to improving the credit score. After 30-60 days Ms. Johnson Credit Score improves. This is a great example of self-improvement.

What Did She Do?

She only spent 30% of her approved $300.00 Credit Limit

She paid her payment before her payment was due

She paid more than the requested payment amount

All correct steps to her credit score

SECOND EXAMPLE

Another example of using your credit card like an American Express Card. Spend 30% and pay the statement and current amount owed bill in full. Pay the Current Balance in full $70.00 this example.

NOTES

Valerie Johnson

9

SAMPLE LETTERS

Inaccurate Info Letter Inaccurate (NAME) or (ADDRESS) or (NOT MY DEBT)

My name is _____. My address is _____. This letter is to tell you inaccurate info is included in my credit report number_____ dated for _____. The last four numbers of my credit report are_____.

Please remove the following inaccurate reporting. It should say _____. Please reply to the address provided. Enclosed is a copy of my state Identification.

Salutation,

Name

Valerie Johnson

NOTES

_____

_____

_____

_____

_____

_____

_____

_____

_____

_____

_____

_____

_____

10

POOR SCORE CREDIT CARDS YOU CAN APPLY TO IN 300 TO 579 FICO SCORES INCLUDING SECURED CARDS

Name Mission Lane Visa LLC
PO BOX 105286
Atlanta, Georgia 30348-5286
https:// www.missionlane.com

Capital One Platinum Secured Credit Card
PO Box 30285
Salt Lake City, UT 84130-0285
Credit One
Request Application Information 1800 752 5493

Discover It Secured Card
POBOX 45909
San Francisco, CA 94145-0909

Premier Credit Card
POBOX 5529
Sioux Falls, SD 57117-5529
800-987-5521

Valerie Johnson

Chase Secure Card
3122 Sheridan Drive Suite 300
Buffalo, New York
800 432 3117

Merrick Bank
POBOX 9201
Old Beth, New York 11804-9001
800 204-5936

Navy Federal
PO BOX 3000
Merrifield, VA 22119-3000
888-842-6328

Total Visa Card
PO Box 84930
Sioux Falls, South Dakota 57118-4930
877=480-6988

Revvi Visa
PO BOX 85800
Sioux Falls, SD 57118-5800
800 845 4804

Milestone MasterCard
Genesis FS Card Services
PO BOX 4477
Beaverton, Oregon 97076-4477
800 305-0330

Petal 1 Visa Credit Card
PO BOX 1150
New York, NY 100008-1150

Reflex MasterCard
PO BOX 3220
Buffalo, New York 14240-3220
866 449 4514

716 Automotive (Car Loan for buying an Automobile)
2618 Bailey Avenue
Buffalo, New York 14215
716 936 9397

Destiny MasterCard
Genesis FS Card Services
PO BOX 477
Beaverton, OR 97076
800 583 5698

First Digital MasterCard
PO BOX 85650
Sioux Falls, SD 57118
844 358 0074

Valerie Johnson

NOTES

Valerie Johnson

11

IMPORTANT TELEPHONE NUMBERS

Sometimes you need someone to provide information to help you Self Improve. In this Credit world we live in sometimes it gets overwhelming. Obtain your goal of improving your credit. Follow the steps included in this Credit Repair Manual, use the sample letters and information and watch your credit score improve in months!

SOME IMPORTANT TELEPHONE NUMBERS

Annual Credit Report and More 1 877 322 8228

Credit Karma 1 888 822 9277
1 800 609 1581

Equifax 1 888 378 4329

Experian 1 888 397 3742

Trans Union 1 800 916 8800

Valerie Johnson

NOTES

12

LESSON ABOUT APR RATES

What is An APR RATES

Average Poor Score APR Rate

Apr Rates For Cars

APR RATES Mortgage

Valerie Johnson

12

LESSON ABOUT APR RATES

What is An APR rate? APR rates are Annual Percentage Rates. APRS determine how much you will pay interest if you carry a balance. On a $1000 balanced paid over 6 months you will spend about $47.00 if your card is a 16% APR. But, the same balance with a 20% balance you will pay about $59.00 in interest over the same period.

Types of APR are fixed or can be variable according to US NEWS. A fixed APR is locked in when you sign up for your credit card and will not change.

A Variable APR can change over time and is usually based on a benchmark rate.

Introductory APR is usually 0% can apply to purchases and balance transfer for an introductory Period.

Penalty APR May apply when your payment is more than 60 days late.

Things are obtainable, but God first who made everything. Work hard at being timely and if you are a first time credit card user. Apply for one. Be faithful over one card, pay more than asked and on time.

Please do not be discouraged because of debt I began with a 498 and was able to obtain a 643 Equifax score. Credit is very important. This world is a credit world sometimes. Some places only take credit cards instead of cash.

This book was meant to encourage you not discourage you. Start paying your bills on time and pay more than asked. Don't try to open up too many new accounts, even if you are able to obtain them. Paying your bills on time and more than ask can become a task if you have too many cards.

Be careful when shopping with your credit cards do not over extend yourself and Buy Now Pay Later the latest in fashion and consumer debt (BNPL) Monthly installment payments must be paid on time Also. So be wise when using credit.

I hope you enjoyed reading this book as much as this Author enjoyed writing and creating. I am thankful and have a heart of Gratitude.

NOTES

Valerie Johnson

ABOUT THE AUTHOR

This Author is a Believer of Jesus Christ. She gave her life to Jesus Christ before the age of 12 and is a member of Salvation Army where she works as an Intake Counselor, does one on one Counseling and teaches life skills. She is blessed to utilize one of her gifts of musicianship, piano and organ at Promise land MBC in Buffalo, New York where she was baptized by Twilius Davis and Pastor Douglas Blakely is Pastor.

This Author Blessed Mom of two Anthony Lowe who is a LPN Nurse and Tiara Johnson who is a Director at a college! Ms. Johnson is also the mom of Eric Johnson who she lovingly called Alex former Supervisor Customer Service of an insurance agency. Alex died of complications due to his Covid in 2022. May he rest in heavenly peace. We miss you.

This Author shares a love of the Holy Bible, Academics, Music and Loves life. She thanks you! Enjoy Reading!

Valerie Johnson

Printed in the United States
by Baker & Taylor Publisher Services